coriander

...makes the difference

Published by Development Dynamics,
Majon, 1a Furze Lane, Purley, Surrey CR83EJ
First published in Great Britain in 2009

ISBN 978-0-9536354-2-9
A catalogue record for this book is available from the British Library.
Printed by MPG Biddles

www.spicemagic.com
www.coriandermakesthedifference.com

coriander

...makes the difference

Dedication

To my mother Sherbanoo Nathani, the essence of elegance and graciousness. And to the memory of my father Salim Nathani, my aunt Mena and my aunt Bulbul—in them I first encountered the qualities that have inspired this book.

Acknowledgements

I would like to thank:

My editors Caroline Curtis & Rhona Kyle, for their enthusiasm and belief in the project and their attention to detail. Clare Meredith, for her artwork & Erroll Jones, for his photography.

Seuly Begum and Fahmida Sultana, the girls from Mulberry School, and their teacher Lee Qun Man—all of whom I would recommend as a sous chef anytime.

Shehzad Lilani, for his humour and his brilliance as a sounding board.

Mike Bokaie, Donna Galbraith & Gemma Rowley, who helped me convert so many of my dreams into reality.

Shamin Ahmed, the very essence of thoughtfulness.

Anar Bhatia, Mamty Gillani, Mehboob and Rozy Fazal, for their special friendship.

My sister Junie, brother Mehmood and sister-in-law Nina, for being there always.

And Mehboob, Kessy, Imraan & Rishad, who have been not only the coriander in my life but much more …

contents

Introduction

Making the Difference 11

The Essentials

Appreciation 15
Kindness 16
Generosity 17
Friendship 18
Integrity 20
Perseverance 22
Enthusiasm 23
Be the Difference 24

Coriander

The Herb Itself 28
Cooking with Coriander 31
Culinary Techniques and Tips 61
Featured Spices 64
Medicinal Benefits 67

The Final Word

Our Contributors Speak 71

making the difference

Sometimes you know that something's missing. Something's not quite right. You've prepared the ingredients and put them together and now the meal is ready to serve. One final taste to check the seasoning, and it's just not right. It needs a little bit extra – but what?

When I left India and came to England, I had never cooked in my life. It was time to learn, and spurred on by my family and friends I did.

Their encouragement made the difference. I did my best, and they added that little bit extra. So too in cooking there is, I think, one ingredient that can have the same effect: coriander. It's a simple ingredient, and it makes all the difference.

The recipes in this collection are simple to prepare. And they use coriander to delicious effect.

And yet, celebrating this herb is not the main purpose behind this book. What I want to celebrate is those little extra bits that can make the difference to us – life's ingredients, if you like.

It may be a quality we can find within ourselves, making a difference to our own endeavours. Enthusiasm, perhaps. Or perseverance, finding the will to carry on. Or integrity, knowing our values and holding on fast.

It may be a quality that we are given. After all, there are times when we cannot do it alone, when other people can make the difference. Their words may show us our value, their kindness lighting up a world gone dark, their friendship bringing us comfort.

All, though, are the qualities that I believe make life palatable. They matter to me above all else, and whenever I come across a proverb or a remark that seems to me to highlight one of these, or to describe it in a new way, I make a note. I now have a considerable collection, and for the first chapter of this book I have selected proverbs from around the world as well as the thoughts of people throughout history – not just those who have made their mark but also those who are less well known.

What, though, would be the point of a book reflecting only my tastes? I want to celebrate not simply the magic that changed my life but also the magic that changed another's. For me, it is so inspiring to know that what we need for ourselves one day is what we are able to give the next. The little bit extra that changed us is the little bit extra we pass on – from one person to the next, from one generation to the next.

So for the final chapter I have asked people to describe what has made, and what makes, the difference to them. I am blessed to count many of these contributors as my friends: they have inspired me, often without realising, and I give thanks to them all. I hope too that their words may be of value to you.

Just as coriander makes the difference, so too did they. And so too can we.

the essentials

appreciation

A smile you sent, will always return.
Indian proverb

Praise the young and they will blossom.
Irish proverb

In critical moments even the very powerful have need of the weakest.
Aesop

Gratitude is not only the greatest of virtues, but the parent of all others.
Cicero

The greatest good you can do for another is not just to share your riches, but to reveal to him his own.
Benjamin Disraeli

The best effect of fine persons is felt after we have left their presence.
Ralph Waldo Emerson

The deepest principle in human nature is the craving to be appreciated.
William James

By appreciating, we make excellence in others our own property.
Voltaire

Feeling gratitude and not expressing it is like wrapping a present and not giving it.
William A. Ward

Gratitude is the sign of noble souls.
Aesop

---

kindness

If you have much, give of your wealth;
if you have little, give of your heart.
Arabic proverb

Deal with the faults of others as gently as with your own.
Chinese proverb

One kind word can warm three winter months.
Japanese proverb

One can pay back the loan of gold, but one dies forever in debt to those who are kind.
Malayan proverb

No act of kindness, no matter how small, is ever wasted.
Aesop

Too often we underestimate the power of a touch, a smile, a kind word, a listening ear, an honest compliment, or the smallest act of caring, all of which have the potential to turn a life around.
Leo Buscaglia

Forget injuries, never forget kindnesses.
Confucius

You cannot do a kindness too soon, for you never know how soon it will be too late.
Ralph Waldo Emerson

If we cannot be clever, we can always be kind.
Alfred Fripp

Wise sayings often fall on barren ground, but a kind word is never thrown away.
Sir Arthur Helps

Be kind, for everyone you meet is fighting a hard battle.
Plato

At times our own light goes out and is rekindled by a spark from another person. Each of us has cause to think with deep gratitude of those who have lighted the flame within us.
Albert Schweitzer

Wherever there is a human being, there is an opportunity for a kindness.
Seneca

Kindness is the language which the deaf can hear and the blind can see.
Mark Twain

The smallest act of kindness is worth more than the grandest intention.
Oscar Wilde

generosity

Real generosity toward the future consists in giving all to what is present.
Albert Camus

Real generosity is doing something nice for someone who will never find out.
Frank A. Clark

Something that has always puzzled me all my life is why, when I am in special need of help, the good deed is usually done by somebody on whom I have no claim.
William Feather

You give but little when you give of your possessions. It is when you give of yourself that you truly give.
Kahlil Gibran

Generosity is giving more than you can, and pride is taking less than you need.
Kahlil Gibran

It is well to give when asked, but it is better to give unasked, through understanding.
Kahlil Gibran

We must give more in order to get more. It is the generous giving of ourselves that produces the generous harvest.
Orison Swett Marden

We should give as we would receive, cheerfully, quickly, and without hesitation; for there is no grace in a benefit that sticks to the fingers.
Seneca

You have not lived a perfect day, even though you have earned your money, unless you have done something for someone who will never be able to repay you.
Ruth Smeltzer

The fragrance always stays in the hand that gives the rose.
Hada Bejar

Generosity is not giving me that which I need more than you do, but it is giving me that which you need more than I do.
Kahlil Gibran

If we should deal out justice only, in this world, who would escape? No, it is better to be generous, and in the end more profitable, for it gains gratitude for us, and love.
Mark Twain

friendship

The road to a friend's house is never long.
Danish proverb

Love me when I least deserve it, because that's when I really need it.
Swedish proverb

I value the friend who for me finds time on his calendar, but I cherish the friend who for me does not consult his calendar.
Robert Brault

Friendship is a strong and habitual inclination in two persons to promote the good and happiness of one another.
Eustace Budgell

I want to be your friend
For ever and ever without break or decay
When the hills are all flat
And the rivers are all dry

When it lightens and thunders
In winter,
When it rains and snows in summer,
When Heaven and Earth mingle
Not till then will I part from you.
Oath of Friendship, Chinese, 1st Century AD

Oh, the comfort – the inexpressible comfort of feeling safe with a person – having neither to weigh thoughts nor measure words, but pouring them all right out, just as they are, chaff and grain together; certain that a faithful hand will take and sift them, keep what is worth keeping, and then with the breath of kindness blow the rest away.
Dinah Craik,
***A Life for a Life*, 1859**

It is one of the blessings of old friends that you can afford to be stupid with them.
Ralph Waldo Emerson

Nothing but heaven itself is better than a friend who is really a friend.

Plautus

Ah, how good it feels! The hand of an old friend.
Henry Wadsworth Longfellow

Each friend represents a world in us, a world possibly not born until they arrive.
Anäis Nin

When we honestly ask ourselves which person in our lives mean the most to us, we often find that it is those who, instead of giving advice, solutions, or cures, have chosen rather to share our pain and touch our wounds with a warm and tender hand. The friend who can be silent with us in a moment of despair or confusion, who can stay with us in an hour of grief and bereavement, who can tolerate now knowing, not curing, not healing and face with us the reality of our powerlessness, that is a friend who cares.
Samuel Paterson

Let us be grateful to people who make us happy, they are the charming gardeners who make our souls blossom.
Marcel Proust

There is one friend in the life of each of us who seems not a separate person, however dear and beloved, but an expansion, an interpretation, of one's self, the very meaning of one's soul.
Edith Wharton

integrity

A wise man makes his own decisions; an ignorant man follows the public opinion.
Chinese proverb

When you were born, you cried and the world rejoiced. Live your life so that when you die, the world cries and you rejoice.
German proverb

Yesterday is but a dream, tomorrow is but a vision. But today well lived makes every yesterday a dream of happiness, and every tomorrow a vision of hope. Look well, therefore, to This Day.
Indian proverb

Do not rejoice at my grief, for when mine is old, yours will be new.
Spanish proverb

Truth and oil always come to the surface.
Spanish proverb

Treat everyone with politeness, even those who are rude to you – not because they are nice, but because you are.
Anonymous

By swallowing evil words unsaid, no one has ever harmed his stomach.
Winston Churchill

Try not to become a man of success but rather to become a man of value.
Albert Einstein

Never criticize a man until you've walked a mile in his moccasins.
Native American proverb

The good man does not grieve that other people do not recognize his merits.
His only anxiety is lest he should fail to recognize theirs.
Confucius

Who you are, what your values are, what you stand for... They are your anchor, your North Star. You won't find them in a book. You'll find them in your soul.
Anne Mulcahy

Life is short but there is always time for courtesy.
Ralph Waldo Emerson, *Social Aims*

Success: To laugh often and much, to win the respect of intelligent people and the affection of children, to earn the appreciation of honest critics and endure the betrayal of false friends, to appreciate beauty, to find the best in others, to leave the world a bit better, whether by a healthy child, a garden patch, or a redeemed social condition; to know even one life has breathed easier because you have lived. This is to have succeeded!
Ralph Waldo Emerson

None of us will ever accomplish anything excellent or commanding except when he listens to this whisper which is heard by him alone.
Ralph Waldo Emerson

It is a greater compliment to be trusted than to be loved.
George Macdonald

I attribute my success to this – I never gave or took any excuse.
Florence Nightingale

For our own success to be real, it must contribute to the success of others.
Eleanor Roosevelt

Regard your good name as the richest jewel you can possibly be possessed of – for credit is like fire; when once you have kindled it you may easily preserve it, but if you once extinguish it, you will find it an arduous task to rekindle it again. The way to gain a good reputation is to endeavor to be what you desire to appear.
Socrates

perseverance

It's not that I'm so smart, it's just that I stay with problems longer.
Albert Einstein

Energy and persistence conquer all things.
Benjamin Franklin

One of the most important principles of success is developing the habit of going the extra mile.
Napoleon Hill

Let me tell you the secret that has led to my goal. My strength lies solely in my tenacity.
Louis Pasteur

Look at a stone cutter hammering away at his rock, perhaps a hundred times without as much as a crack showing in it. Yet at the hundred-and-first blow it will split in two, and I know it was not the last blow that did it, but all that had gone before.
Jacob A. Riis

The greatest glory in living lies not in never falling, but in rising every time we fall.
Nelson Mandela

Success is not measured by what you accomplish but by the opposition you have encountered, and the courage with which you have maintained the struggle against overwhelming odds.
Orison Swett Marden

enthusiasm

By asking for the impossible we obtain the possible.
Italian proverb

Success is to go from one failure to another with no loss of enthusiasm.
Winston Churchill

Wherever you go, go with all your heart.
Confucius

Never underestimate the power of passion.
Eve Sawyer

Nothing ever succeeds which exuberant spirits have not helped to produce.
Nietzsche

---

be the difference

One generation plants the trees; another gets the shade.
Chinese proverb

Only those who dare to fail greatly can ever achieve greatly.
Robert F. Kennedy

Let no one ever come to you without leaving better and happier.
Mother Teresa

Nobody made a greater mistake than he who did nothing because he could only do a little.
Edmund Burke

The world is moved along, not only by the mighty shoves of its heroes, but also by the aggregate of tiny pushes of each honest worker.
Helen Keller

Each time a man stands up for an ideal, or acts to improve the lot of others, or strikes out against injustice, he sends forth a tiny ripple of hope... and crossing each other from a million different centers of energy and daring those ripples build a current that can sweep down the mightiest walls of oppression and resistance.
Robert F. Kennedy

The first question which the priest and the Levite asked was: "If I stop to help this man, what will happen to me?" But... the good Samaritan reversed the question: "If I do not stop to help this man, what will happen to him?"
Martin Luther King, Jr.

Everybody can be great. Because anybody can serve. You don't have to have a college degree to serve. You don't have to make your subject and your verb agree to serve.... You don't have to know the second theory of thermodynamics in physics to serve. You only need a heart full of grace. A soul generated by love.
Martin Luther King, Jr.

Never doubt that a small group of thoughtful, committed citizens can change the world. Indeed, it is the only thing that ever has.
Margaret Mead

If you can't feed a hundred people, then feed just one.
Mother Teresa

I expect to pass through life but once. If therefore, there be any kindness I can show, or any good thing I can do to any fellow being, let me do it now, and not defer or neglect it, as I shall not pass this way again.
William Penn

I am of the opinion that my life belongs to the whole community and as long as I live, it is my privilege to do for it whatever I can. I want to be thoroughly used up when I die. For the harder I work the more I live. ... Life is no brief candle to me. It's a splendid torch which I've got to hold up for the moment and I want to make it burn as brightly as possible before handing it on to future generations.
George Bernard Shaw

Dare to reach out your hand into the darkness, to pull another hand into the light.
Norman B. Rice

In about the same degree as you are helpful, you will be happy.
Karl Reiland

Wherever a man turns he can find someone who needs him.
Albert Schweitzer

The great French **Marshal Lyautey** once asked his gardener to plant a tree. The gardener objected that the tree was slow-growing and would not reach maturity for 100 years. The Marshal replied, 'In that case, there is no time to lose!'

coriander

the herb itself

History

A native of the Mediterranean and Middle East regions, coriander (or *cilantro* as it is known in the Americas) was probably one of the first herbs and spices used by mankind. There is evidence, in fact, of the plant's existence as far back as 5000 BC. The ancient Egyptians cultivated and commonly used this herb - and coriander seeds have been found in Egyptian tombs. It crops up in Sanskrit writings dating from about 1500 BC and it was also popular with the ancient Greeks. Like the Egyptians, they prized it for its medicinal as well as its culinary uses. It even merits a mention in the Bible's Old Testament, where 'manna' is described as 'like coriander seed, white'. Coriander was first brought to Britain by the Romans, who were also responsible for spreading it throughout Europe. And it was one of the first spices to arrive in America.

The Latin name coriandrum is thought to be derived from the Greek koros (a bedbug) because of the unpleasant, foetid smell of the leaves. As a stimulant and spice, and for its healing properties, it has been cultivated widely throughout many regions of the world. It was also traditionally reputed to be an aphrodisiac.

A herb or a spice?

Extensively grown in India, Russia, Central Europe, North Africa, South America and South and Western Australia, the coriander plant yields two primary products used for culinary purposes: the fresh green herb and the spice. The latter is the dried form of the whole mature seed capsule (fruit), commercially known as coriander seed. The odour and flavour of these two products are markedly different. The herb is used to add flavour to dishes in Asia, the Middle East and Central and South America, while the fruits are an important ingredient of curry powder. They are also used as a pickling spice, in seasonings and sausages, as well as in pastries, bread, buns, cakes and other confectionery.

Culinary uses

Coriander, when used as a garnish, contributes to making a meal attractive and appetising. The coriander leaves look a bit like flat-leaf Italian parsley and, in fact, the two plants are related. The leaves have a similar shape and they are both best eaten raw, as the flavour diminishes after cooking. In both plants, the root tastes similar to the leaves, and its flavour tolerates boiling or simmering much better. As a result of these similarities, coriander is sometimes known as Chinese or Indian parsley.

In the Middle East, coriander leaves are used in pickles, curries, and chutneys. In Latin America (especially Mexico), the Caribbean and the southwest of the United States, they are used in everything from salsas and salads to burritos or meat dishes. And, of course, coriander leaves are popular in most parts of Asia. In India, they are widely used in many different regional dishes. They are considered indispensable in Thailand (both the root and the leaves are needed for green curry paste), Vietnam and parts of China, where the chopped leaves appear as a garnish on almost every dish (sometimes combined with or substituted for peppermint or Vietnamese coriander).

Buying and storing

Fresh coriander is widely available in supermarkets all year round. The best way to store it is to place it in a tumbler or glass bottle, filled with cold water to cover the bottom of the stems, and keep it in the refrigerator; it will last much longer this way. If you have bought a very large quantity, chop it all and keep it in an airtight container in the freezer, adding however much you need to the dish during cooking (as opposed to scattering it over the cooked dish just before serving). However, be warned – frozen coriander leaves do not have the same flavour as fresh.

Coriander seeds may be lightly roasted to enhance the flavour and then stored in an airtight container for up to one year.

Ground coriander will keep for 4–6 months if stored in an airtight container. Whenever possible, however, you should use whole coriander seeds instead of ground coriander because the latter loses its flavour more quickly. It is not difficult to grind coriander seeds with a mortar and pestle when you need them. Personally, though, I use a small coffee grinder for grinding all my spices; it's much easier. If you're going to follow my lead, bear in mind that I have two grinders – one for coffee and one for spices only. Trust me: coffee and spices don't mix!

Nutritional notes

Coriander fruits contain volatile oil, lipids, starch, pectins, minerals and essential fatty acids. Coriander leaves are a good source of vitamin A, C, K, thiamin, riboflavin, folic acid, calcium, iron, magnesium and potassium. They also contain small amounts of niacin, vitamin B6 and zinc.

Medicinal benefits

Coriander is regarded as one of the major medicinal herbs. Coriander seeds are said to be beneficial as an appetite stimulant, as well as having sedative and carminative properties. They are reputed to help with muscular and abdominal pains, including bloating and flatulence, and to reduce digestive spasms. In Iran, coriander has traditionally been used to relieve anxiety and insomnia, and it is widely regarded as being good for the nervous system. It is also considered useful as a general bactericide and fungicide. Modern phytotherapeutics recommends coriander seeds as beneficial for treating: anorexia, dyspepsia, intestinal worms, hypogalactic mothers, dysfunctions of the mammary glands and abdominal pains. They are also reputed to be beneficial for conjunctivitis, as a diuretic, and for allergies, skin rashes and acne.

cooking with coriander

menu

All recipes serve 2

Fusilli with chilli, artichokes and olives
Teriyaki salmon
Chicken with black bean, peppers and chilli
Potatoes with cumin and tomatoes
Chickpeas with spinach
Fish cakes
Vegetable couscous
Carrot and coriander soup
Salad of artichokes, olives and beans with pesto
Garlic spinach
Black-eyed beans
Spring vegetable omelette
Cumin rice
Mince with spinach
Green beans with cumin and garlic
Prawns with creamy pasta
Filet mignon à la Mikal
Chicken pilau
Pan-fried fish with charred garlic
Asparagus and coriander risotto

fusilli with chilli, artichokes and olives

The versatility of pasta never ceases to amaze me. The most important rules are not to overcook it and also to toss it only briefly into the sauce, so it retains its flavour.

200g/7oz/1¾ cups fusilli
3 tablespoons olive oil
400g/14oz canned artichoke hearts
4 garlic cloves, peeled and finely chopped
1 red chilli, chopped
400g/14 oz canned chopped tomatoes
1 tablespoon tomato purée (paste)
200g (7oz) pitted black olives
150g/5oz mozzarella cheese, cut into cubes
50g/2oz/½ cup freshly grated Grana Padano cheese
handful finely chopped fresh coriander (cilantro) leaves
salt

First cook the fusilli in a large pan with plenty of boiling salted water according to the instructions on the pack. (It should be *al dente* – cooked but firm to the bite.)

Three minutes before the pasta is due to be ready, heat the oil in a frying pan, then add the artichoke hearts, garlic, red chilli, chopped tomatoes and tomato purée (paste), then stir over a medium heat for about 2 minutes. Add the olives and mozzarella. Drain the fusilli thoroughly, then return to the pan. Pour over the sauce and mix together gently. Serve immediately, garnished with the Grana Padano and coriander (cilantro).

teriyaki salmon

The only dish that I have managed to teach my sons! I believe they have it three times a week. It is delicious, simple and healthy! If you are able to splash out, black cod is amazing cooked in this way.

2 salmon fillets, weighing about 250g/9oz in total
2 tablespoons teriyaki sauce
handful finely chopped fresh coriander (cilantro) leaves

Place the salmon fillets on a microwavable plate, then pour over the sauce and set aside for 5 minutes. Cover with microwavable clingfilm, then put the salmon in the microwave on full power for 3 minutes. Serve garnished with the coriander (cilantro).

chicken with black bean, peppers and chilli

Chinese dishes like this one should be cooked over a very high heat to seal in the taste of the ingredients and add flavour. Don't be tempted to add salt – both the black bean paste and soy sauce are quite salty. This is best served with plain boiled rice, or cumin rice (see page 53) if you want a fusion meal.

3 tablespoons oil for shallow frying
7cm/3in piece fresh ginger, peeled and finely sliced
400g/14oz chicken breast, diced
1 medium onion, peeled and sliced
1 red chilli, sliced
2 tablespoons black bean paste
2 tablespoons dark soy sauce
1 red (bell) pepper, deseeded and sliced
1 green (bell) pepper, deseeded and sliced
handful finely chopped fresh coriander (cilantro) leaves

Heat a wok over a high heat until smoke rises, then add the oil. Now add the ginger and chicken in quick succession. Stir around for 5 minutes, or until the chicken is speckled brown. Add the onion and chilli and stir-fry for a further 2 minutes. Then add the black bean paste and soy sauce, and continue to cook for 2 minutes. Finally, add the (bell) peppers and cook for another 2 minutes. The peppers should be crisp but not too well done. Garnish with the coriander (cilantro) and serve.

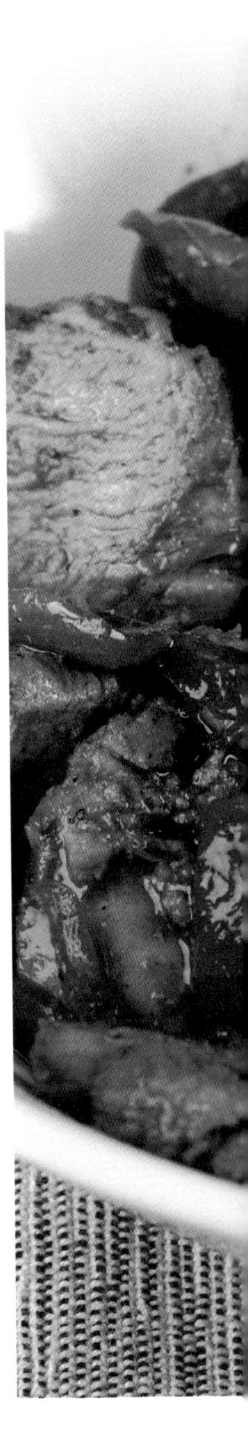

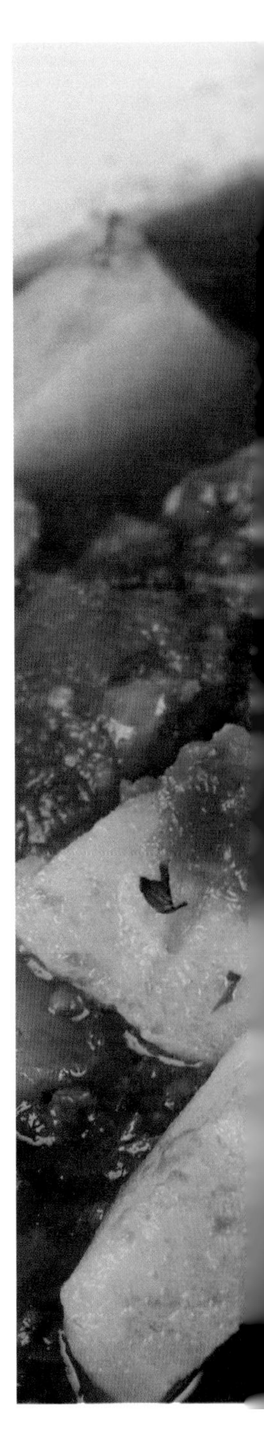

potatoes with cumin and tomatoes

This has always been a family favourite. In India, we had it only in winter, when tomatoes were plentiful. Served with puris (a deep-fried Indian bread), it is a great hit with children. It is also delicious served as an accompaniment to roast chicken, lamb chops or fish.

4 medium potatoes, weighing about 750g/1lb 10oz
2 tablespoons oil, for shallow frying
2 garlic cloves, peeled and chopped
1 tablespoon cumin seeds
¼ teaspoon turmeric
¼ teaspoon chilli powder
400g/14oz canned chopped tomatoes
handful finely chopped fresh coriander (cilantro) leaves
salt

First boil the potatoes in their skins in a pan of boiling salted water until really soft. Drain and allow to cool a little, then peel the skin off using your fingers – not a knife – and set aside.

In a deep frying pan or nonstick wok, heat the oil, then add the garlic and cook over a high heat (but not too hot, or the garlic will burn), stirring continuously, for 10 seconds, or until browned at the edges. Now add the cumin seeds and potatoes in quick succession, followed by the turmeric, chilli powder and tomatoes. Add salt to taste and cook over a medium heat for 5 minutes, stirring frequently. To serve, garnish with the coriander (cilantro).

chickpeas with spinach

I stumbled upon this dish by accident when I did not have enough chickpeas to create a meal. The addition of spinach creates a wonderful contrast, not only by adding colour, but also by transforming the texture. If you prefer, you can make this with fresh tomatoes, but the canned variety give a great colour.

2 tablespoons oil for shallow frying
4–5 curry leaves
1 teaspoon mustard seeds
1 teaspoon puréed ginger
1 teaspoon puréed garlic/5 garlic cloves, peeled and crushed
½ teaspoon turmeric
½ teaspoon chilli powder
100g/3½oz canned chopped tomatoes
400g canned chickpeas, drained
200g/7oz/3⁄4 cup frozen chopped spinach
handful finely chopped fresh coriander (cilantro) leaves
salt

In a large frying pan or nonstick wok, heat the oil and, when it is hot, drop in a curry leaf. If it sizzles and turns a darker shade, add all the other leaves. If the leaf turns very dark, reduce the heat and add the remaining leaves after 1 minute. Add the mustard seeds, ginger, garlic, turmeric, chilli powder and chopped tomatoes. Stir for a couple of minutes, then add salt to taste. Now add the chickpeas and spinach. Stir and leave to cook over a medium heat for 10 minutes, or until the spinach is cooked and combined with the chickpeas. Garnish with the coriander (cilantro) before serving.

fish cakes

I love fish cakes and this is such an easy, tasty recipe that it's worth making an extra batch to stash away in the freezer for standby lunches or after-work suppers. You can easily adapt the recipe to use crab meat, tuna or cod, if you prefer. The fish cakes are fabulous served with a mint chutney.

350g/12 oz canned red salmon
350g/12oz potatoes, peeled, boiled and mashed
2 handfuls finely chopped fresh coriander (cilantro) leaves
1 green chilli, finely chopped, or ¼ teaspoon chilli powder
1 garlic clove, peeled and finely chopped
3 spring onions (scallions), trimmed and finely chopped
2 teaspoons Worcester sauce
1 tablespoon mayonnaise
½ teaspoon English mustard
1 medium egg, beaten
1 tablespoon oil for shallow frying
salt and freshly ground black pepper to taste

In a large bowl, mix all the ingredients apart from the oil together thoroughly with a wooden spoon. Then, using your hands, make the mixture into 8 round patties. Put on a plate, then cover with clingfilm (plastic wrap) and chill in the refrigerator for 30 minutes.

In a nonstick frying pan, heat the oil and cook the fish cakes over a high heat for about 5 minutes, turning them carefully – so they retain their shape – from time to time, until speckled brown. Serve immediately.

vegetable couscous

Couscous is great served warm or cold, and makes an equally good light supper dish or accompaniment. If you want to make it more substantial, stir 1 large roasted chicken breast, cut into strips, into the finished dish. Either way, it is delicious – the flavour of garlic always combines brilliantly with pepper and olive oil.

2 tablespoons olive oil
1 green (bell) pepper, deseeded and chopped into 2.5cm/1in squares
1 red (bell) pepper, deseeded and chopped into 2.5cm/1in squares
2 medium carrots, finely sliced into rounds
1 medium red onion, peeled and coarsely chopped
2 garlic cloves, peeled and finely chopped
100g/3½ oz/½ cup couscous
handful finely chopped fresh coriander (cilantro) leaves
¼ teaspoon salt

In a large frying pan, heat the oil, then add both the (bell) peppers, the carrots and the onion, and cook over a medium heat for 5–7 minutes, stirring occasionally. Add the garlic and cook for a further 1 minute. Remove from the heat and set aside.

Place the couscous in a heatproof bowl, then add the salt and cover with boiling water. Set aside for about 2 minutes to allow the couscous to absorb the water.

Add the couscous to the vegetables, then return to a medium heat and cook for 2 minutes, stirring gently. Serve garnished with the coriander (cilantro).

carrot and coriander soup

This is a recent addition to my repertoire of soup recipes. It has a wonderfully rich flavour, resulting from the use of a good stock, jazzed up with garlic and fresh coriander (cilantro). Serve with warm French bread or ciabatta and, for a special touch when entertaining, top the soup with a swirl of single (light) cream.

5cm/2in piece ginger
3–4 chicken bones
2 small shallots, peeled and finely chopped
5 medium carrots, diced
1 garlic clove, peeled and finely chopped
handful finely chopped fresh coriander (cilantro) leaves
¼ teaspoon salt and freshly ground black pepper

Place the ginger, chicken bones, shallots, carrots, garlic and salt in a large pan together with 1.2 litres/2 pints/5 cups of boiling water. Return to the boil, then cover with a tightly fitting lid and simmer gently for about 25 minutes, or until the carrots are really soft. (If you prefer, you can make the soup in a pressure cooker, which will take only 5 minutes.) Remove from the heat and discard the chicken bones and ginger.

Place the soup in a food processor or liquidiser and whizz until smooth. Add freshly ground black pepper to taste and garnish with the coriander (cilantro), then serve immediately.

salad of artichokes, olives and beans with pesto

An easy-to-prepare salad that looks stunning. The medley of colours is a feast for the eyes and the wonderful flavour of pesto means it is guaranteed to go down a treat.

200g/7oz whole green beans, trimmed
400g/14 oz canned artichokes
200g/7oz pitted black olives
6 cherry tomatoes
¼ cucumber, diced
1 red (bell) pepper, deseeded and diced
4 asparagus spears, chopped into 5cm/2in pieces
100g/3½oz feta cheese, cut into cubes
1 tablespoon extra virgin olive oil
2 garlic cloves, peeled and crushed
2 tablespoons pesto sauce
handful finely chopped fresh coriander (cilantro) leaves

Blanch the beans in a pan of boiling salted water for 2 minutes. Drain and set aside to cool.

In a large serving dish, mix together the beans, artichokes, olives, tomatoes, cucumber, pepper, asparagus and feta cheese. In a medium bowl, whisk together the olive oil, garlic and pesto sauce, then pour the dressing over the salad. Toss well to mix and serve garnished with the coriander (cilantro).

garlic spinach

I would be totally lost without garlic – its seductive flavour transforms any dish, and this is an easy way of making spinach really splendid. Make sure you taste the spinach before serving, to make sure you have added enough salt. When cooking spicy dishes, more rather than less salt is needed to bring the flavours out.

2 tablespoons olive oil
1 medium onion, peeled and finely chopped
2 garlic cloves, peeled and finely chopped
200g/7oz/generous ¾ cup frozen chopped spinach
handful finely chopped fresh coriander (cilantro) leaves
salt

In a large frying pan, heat the oil, then add the onion – it should sizzle. Immediately lower the heat to medium and cook, stirring continuously, until browned at the edges. Add the garlic, and cook for about 10 seconds, stirring continuously, until slightly browned. Then add the spinach, together with salt to taste, and leave to cook over a medium heat for 5–7 minutes, stirring occasionally, until soft. To serve, garnish with the coriander (cilantro).

black-eyed beans

Beans are a great source of protein, and this mouthwatering dish is transformed by the infusion of garlic and cumin seeds dropped into hot oil. If you put the beans in water to soak before going to work, they'll be ready to cook when you get home. And to save more time, cook the beans in a pressure cooker – they will take only 10 minutes.

250g/9oz/2¼ cups black-eyed beans (black-eye peas)
5cm/2in piece ginger
½ teaspoon salt
2 tablespoons oil for shallow frying
1 garlic clove, peeled and finely chopped
1 tablespoon cumin seeds
handful finely chopped fresh coriander (cilantro) leaves

Begin by soaking the beans in plenty of cold water for 2 hours, then drain. In a large pan of boiling water, cook the beans, together with the ginger and salt, for 30 minutes, or until they are really soft. The beans should now be fairly dry, with only about 125ml/4fl oz/½ cup of water remaining. Set aside.

Next, in a small frying pan, heat the oil. It needs to be really hot – test by dropping a piece of the chopped garlic in and, if it sizzles, add the remaining garlic. It should brown at the edges very quickly. Now add the cumin seeds – they will sizzle immediately – and then tip this mixture into the beans and stir gently to mix. Return the beans to the boil and simmer gently for 5 minutes. Garnish with the coriander (cilantro) before serving.

spring vegetable omelette

My grandmother made the best spicy omelettes (omelets) by adding hot green chillies, cumin and coriander (cilantro) to the mixture. We also ate omelettes with curry sauce and rice! If you don't have coriander-cumin powder, just use ½ teaspoon of coriander powder and ½ teaspoon of cumin powder. You can serve this either folded into an omelette or flat like a tortilla.

3 tablespoons oil for shallow frying
3 asparagus spears, cut into 2.5cm/1in pieces
3 spring onions (scallions), trimmed and finely chopped
1 medium tomato, finely chopped
1 green chilli, finely chopped
½ green (bell) pepper, deseeded and finely chopped
2 garlic cloves, peeled and finely chopped
115g/4oz/1 cup frozen sweetcorn (corn)
handful finely chopped fresh coriander (cilantro) leaves
1 teaspoon coriander-cumin powder
¼ teaspoon chilli powder
3 medium eggs, beaten
salt

In a frying pan, heat 2 tablespoons of the oil and add the asparagus, spring onions (scallions), tomato, green chilli, (bell) pepper, garlic, sweetcorn (corn) and coriander (cilantro). Cook over a medium heat for about 5 minutes, stirring frequently, until the vegetables are soft. Add salt to taste, the coriander-cumin powder and the chilli powder, then stir and cook for a further 2–3 minutes. Remove from the heat and transfer to a bowl, then fold the eggs into the vegetables.

In a medium frying pan, heat the remaining oil and add the omelette mixture. Cook over a low heat for 5-7 minutes, or until the eggs are cooked through. Serve immediately.

cumin rice

From fragrant pilaus to scented saffron risottos – the aroma of rice is always irresistible. Infused with cumin, this accompaniment is simple to make and tastes wonderful with almost any dish.

250g/9oz/1¼ cups basmati rice
2 tablespoons oil for shallow frying
1 tablespoon cumin seeds
5cm/2in stick cinnamon
2 cloves
2 cardamom pods
2 bay leaves
½ teaspoon salt
handful finely chopped fresh coriander (cilantro) leaves

Begin by soaking the rice in plenty of cold water for 30 minutes. Drain into a sieve (strainer) and rinse under cold running water until the water runs clear, then set aside.

In a large pan, heat the oil and, once hot, add the cumin seeds, cinnamon, cloves, cardamom pods and bay leaves in quick succession. Immediately add the rice and stir gently, taking care not to break the grains. Add the salt and 425ml/¾ pint/generous 1¾ cups of boiling water. Return to the boil, then reduce the heat to its lowest setting and cover with a tightly fitting lid. Leave to cook for 10 minutes without removing the lid. To serve, garnish with the coriander (cilantro).

mince with spinach

This has a wonderful combination of flavours and is great served with rice, naan or pitta (pita) bread. For a lunchtime option, you could even roll it into a tortilla and garnish with salad. If you don't have coriander-cumin powder, use 1 tablespoon of coriander powder and 1 tablespoon of cumin powder.

6 tablespoons oil
2 medium onions, peeled and finely chopped
450g/1lb/4 cups minced (ground) beef
2 teaspoons freshly ground garlic
2 teaspoons freshly ground ginger
2 tablespoons coriander-cumin powder
½ teaspoon turmeric
½ teaspoon chilli powder
1 teaspoon tomato purée (paste)
2 each of cloves, cardamom pods, small sticks of cinnamon and dried bay leaves (whole garam masala)
200g/7oz/¾ cup frozen chopped spinach
handful of finely chopped fresh coriander (cilantro) leaves
salt, to taste

In a large frying pan or nonstick wok, heat the oil, then cook the onions over a medium heat, stirring occasionally, until brown. Add the mince (ground beef) and cook over a high heat for 2 minutes, to brown. Now add all the other ingredients apart from the spinach and coriander (cilantro). Cook over a high heat, stirring constantly, and adding water 1 tablespoonful at a time to make sure the spices do not burn (this is called bhunaoing). Continue cooking in this way – as soon as the water has been absorbed, adding another tablespoonful – for at least 10 minutes.

Now add 600ml/20fl oz/2½ cups water and leave to simmer over a very low heat for about 15 minutes, or until the mince (ground beef) is cooked. There should be very little liquid left at the end. If necessary, turn up the heat and bubble to reduce the liquid. Then add the spinach and leave to cook for another 5 minutes. Garnish with the coriander (cilantro) and serve.

green beans with cumin and garlic

This is a really simple way of transforming green beans into something special. The recipe can be adapted to suit other vegetables, if you like. Or try throwing a few chopped asparagus spears into the beans for a wonderful variation.

200g/7oz green beans, trimmed
1 tablespoon oil, for shallow frying
2 garlic cloves, peeled and finely chopped
2 teaspoons cumin seeds
handful finely chopped fresh coriander (cilantro) leaves
salt

First simmer the green beans in a medium pan of boiling salted water for 2 minutes. Drain and set aside. Now heat the oil in a medium frying pan, then add the garlic and cook over a high heat (but not too hot or the garlic will burn), stirring, for 10 seconds, or until browned at the edges. Add the cumin seeds, green beans and salt to taste, then stir to mix and heat through for a couple of minutes. Taste to check there is enough salt, then garnish with the coriander (cilantro) and serve.

prawns with creamy pasta

This is a rich and deliciously decadent pasta dish – ideal if you want to forget about calories for the day and indulge in an unashamedly luscious treat.

200g/7oz/1¾ cups penne or farfalle
115g/4oz/¾ cup green beans, trimmed and halved
115g/4oz/1 cup frozen peas
½ tablespoon butter
1 garlic clove, peeled and finely chopped
225g/8oz cooked large king prawns (jumbo shrimp)
150ml/5fl oz/ 2/3 cup double (heavy) cream
25g/1oz/¼ cup freshly grated Parmesan
handful finely chopped fresh coriander (cilantro) leaves
salt and freshly ground black pepper

Cook the pasta in a large pan of boiling salted water according to the instructions on the pack. Five minutes before the end of the cooking time, add the beans and peas. When the pasta is cooked, drain and set aside. (It should be *al dente* – cooked but firm to the bite).

In a large frying pan, melt the butter, then add the garlic and prawns (shrimp) and heat through. Now add the prawns (shrimp) and garlic to the pasta and vegetables, then toss gently to mix and stir in the cream. Sprinkle over black pepper to taste along with the Parmesan, and garnish with the coriander (cilantro).

filet mignon à la mikal

French for an 'exquisite or dainty fillet', this cut of beef is so tender that it should never be cooked beyond medium-rare. The longer you cook it, the less tender and more dry it becomes. My nephew Mikal, who is only 12, has a most discerning palate and enjoys ordering the finest cuts of meat when we go to restaurants. After looking at the prices, however, he will say, 'I'd better not have that'. At this point he knows that, if his parents are not there, we will say, 'Have what you want!' Mikal loves Wagyu beef, but settles for Filet mignon! This dish is one I have dedicated to him. He recommends serving it with a green salad drizzled with extra virgin olive oil and balsamic vinegar.

2 filet mignon steaks – a type of fillet (tenderloin) steak, about 2.5cm/1in thick, weighing about 225g/8oz in total
1 tablespoon Worcestershire sauce
1 tablespoon soy sauce
1 garlic clove, peeled and finely chopped
1 tablespoon finely chopped fresh coriander (cilantro) leaves
25g/1oz/¼ stick butter
pinch freshly ground black pepper
salt to taste

Place the steaks in a bowl with the Worcestershire sauce, soy sauce, garlic and coriander (cilantro). Cover and leave to marinate in the refrigerator for at least 2 hours.

Heat the butter in a stainless steel frying pan (do not use a nonstick one – stainless steel reaches a higher temperature, so it seals the flavour better and gives a more browned appearance). When the butter is really hot, put the steaks in – they should sizzle and smoke. Cook the steaks for 2 minutes on either side for rare and a further minute on each side for medium rare. Add the black pepper and salt to taste (soy sauce is very salty, so this may not be necessary). Serve immediately.

chicken pilau

Fragrant pilaus are a hot favourite in most Indian homes. The chicken, rice and aromatic spices combine to transform a simple dish into something really delicious. And using chicken on the bone makes this pilau much more flavoursome. Serve with raita (an Indian yogurt relish) made by beating plain yogurt and adding grated cucumber and chopped coriander (cilantro) leaves.

250g/9oz/1¼ cups basmati rice
3 tablespoons oil for shallow frying
2 medium onions, peeled and finely chopped
1 tablespoon cumin seeds
400g/14oz chicken on the bone
1 medium potato, peeled and cut into quarters
2 medium tomatoes, finely chopped
1 teaspoon puréed ginger
1 teaspoon puréed garlic/5 garlic cloves, peeled and crushed
2 each of cardamom pods, cinnamon sticks, bay leaves and cloves (whole garam masala)
handful of finely chopped fresh coriander (cilantro) leaves
salt

First soak the rice in plenty of cold water for 30 minutes. Then drain and rinse in a sieve (strainer) under cold running water until the water runs clear.

In a large pan, heat the oil and cook the onions over a medium heat until browned at the edges. Add the cumin seeds, followed quickly by the chicken and potato, and stir for a couple of minutes. Then add the tomatoes, ginger, garlic, whole garam masala and salt to taste. Add 850ml/1½ pints/3¾ cups of boiling water from a kettle and return to the boil. Cover with a tightly fitting lid and simmer gently over a low heat until the chicken and potatoes are cooked (about 15 minutes).

Now add the rice and the coriander (cilantro). At this stage, make sure the water level is 2.5cm/1in above the level of the rice – top up with boiling water from the kettle if necessary. Return to the boil, then immediately turn the heat to its lowest setting and cover with a tightly fitting lid. Leave to cook for 10 minutes without opening the lid – this would allow steam to escape and affect the way the rice cooks. Serve immediately.

pan-fried fish with charred garlic

I love using tilapia for this recipe even though I am aware that more sophisticated fish-lovers may sneer! The charring of the garlic transforms the fish into something truly sublime.

2 teaspoons olive oil
3 garlic cloves, peeled and finely chopped
2 cod or tilapia fillets
handful finely chopped fresh coriander (cilantro) leaves
salt and freshly ground black pepper

In a frying pan, heat the oil and, when it is hot, add the garlic – it should turn brown quickly. (This is what gives the fish its wonderful flavour.) Now lower the heat to medium, then add the fish and pan-fry for 7 minutes, turning carefully once or twice. Add salt and freshly ground pepper to taste, and garnish with the coriander (cilantro). Serve immediately.

asparagus and coriander risotto

My favourite risotto rice is arborio – a large, round grain that develops a lovely creamy texture when cooked. And the trick to making a great risotto is to use good stock and decent wine. Also, don't add more liquid until all of it has been absorbed. If you like, you could add some prawns (shrimp) or, if you are feeling extravagant, a spoonful of caviar!

50g/2oz/½ stick butter
1 medium onion, peeled and finely chopped
350g/12oz/generous 1½ cups arborio risotto rice
200ml/7fl oz/generous ¾ cup dry white wine
1.2 litres/2 pints/5 cups chicken stock, fresh or made with stock cubes
6 asparagus spears, cut into 2.5cm/1in pieces
55g/2oz/½ cup freshly grated Parmesan cheese, plus a few shavings to garnish
handful finely chopped fresh coriander (cilantro) leaves
dried chilli flakes, to garnish
salt and freshly ground black pepper

In a large pan, melt the butter and cook the onion over a low heat until soft. Add the rice and stir the grains around for 1 minute – do not let them brown. Then add the wine and keep stirring the rice over a medium heat until it has all been absorbed. Now add the stock, a ladleful at a time, stirring continuously until it has been absorbed before adding the next ladleful. Continue doing this until all the stock has been used. The risotto should be firm and creamy.

Remove the pan from the heat and add the asparagus, grated Parmesan and most of the coriander (cilantro). Add seasoning to taste, then stir and set aside for 5 minutes. Serve garnished with the remaining coriander (cilantro), Parmesan shavings and chilli flakes.

culinary techniques and tips

Preparing puréed ginger and puréed garlic

Several recipes in this book call for these two ingredients, and it is as important to make sure they are puréed as it is to use fresh spices. However, puréeing small quantities of ginger and garlic can be time-consuming, so here I have included chilling and freezing instructions in the methods for each.

To make 8 tablespoons puréed ginger: Take 200g/7oz of fresh ginger. Peel, wash and cut it into pieces. Place the pieces in a food processor, or in a pestle and mortar, with 4 tablespoons water and blend, or crush, until you have a smooth paste. Stir in 1 teaspoon oil to help preserve the paste, and refrigerate. This will keep in the refrigerator for up to 7 days. You can also freeze individual portions in an ice-cube tray, to use as and when you need them. This can be frozen for up to 2 months.

To make 8 tablespoons of puréed garlic: Take 200g/7oz of garlic cloves. Peel the cloves, place them in a food processor, or in a pestle and mortar, with 4 tablespoons water and blend, or crush, until you have a fine paste. Stir in 1 teaspoon oil, to help preserve the paste, and refrigerate. This will keep in the refrigerator for up to 7 days. You can also freeze individual portions in an ice-cube tray, to use as and when you need them. This can be frozen for up to 2 months.

Bhunaoing

This is the process of cooking spices at a high temperature and adding tablespoons of water, stock or yogurt to lower the temperature and prolong the time the spices can be cooked without burning and drying out.

The reasoning behind this technique is to allow the spices to blend together so as not to taste raw or catch the throat. This technique is the key to Mogul cooking, and it requires patience and practice. As you *bhunao*, you will notice the oil start to separate from the spices: this is the sign that the spices have blended properly.

Coriander-cumin powder

Where I have mentioned coriander-cumin powder in this book, I refer to a powder called *dhania-jeera* in India, which is simply a combination of coriander powder and cumin powder. If you use both powders separately and in the correct proportions (ie half of each), the end result will be the same.

Garam masala

Garam masala literally means 'hot spices'. It is a mixture of several different spices, and many people make their own powder at home with different combinations, sometimes including spices such as mace, peppercorns and nutmeg. In its powdered form, it should be used very sparingly and only at the end of preparing a dish, usually as a garnish. Garam masala spices used whole (eg whole cloves, bay leaves, cinnamon sticks and cardamom pods) add a wonderful warmth and richness to food and can be added from the beginning of cooking. The less edible elements of whole garam masala, such as cinnamon sticks, can be fished out by the cook at the end of cooking, though in India they are generally left in and discreetly removed by each diner to the side of their plate should they happen to find any in their portion.

Oil

Corn oil is my favourite and the oil I would recommend for all the recipes in this book. When using the *bhunao* technique, it is advisable to be generous with the oil, as this helps to amalgamate the spices. If there is too much extra oil floating on the surface of the dish once it is cooked, it can be easily removed with a spoon.

Rice

Rice should be stored in a cool place and should always be soaked for 30 minutes before using, then rinsed out several times under cold running water in order to remove the starch, which is what makes it sticky.

Spoonfuls

All spoonfuls are level.

featured spices

Bay leaf: Strongly aromatic; can be used fresh or dried. When added to hot oil, releases its full flavour. Adds a wonderful aroma to rice and meat preparations.

Cardamom: An ancient ingredient said to have grown in the Hanging Gardens of Babylon. Adds aroma and fragrance to dishes. Available in pods (green or black), as loose seeds or powder. My own preference is for the green pods. One of the ingredients in *garam masala* (a spice mixture used in many Indian dishes).

Cinnamon: Another ancient ingredient. Once a rare and expensive spice; said to have been used by Moses to anoint the Ark of the Covenant. Today it is widely available and affordable and used for its flavour and the aroma it imparts to meat and rice dishes. Available in sticks or powdered form; the stick used whole imparts more flavour and can be discarded once the dish is ready (it is not meant to be eaten).

Cloves: The dried unopened buds of the clove tree. Used in cooking, medicine and for making perfume.

Coriander (cilantro) leaves: My favourite herb. Fresh green coriander leaves are a welcome addition to every Indian dish. They should always be very finely chopped when used to garnish dishes, to release the full flavour. Ground with mint and chillies, they make a wonderful marinade or basis for a sauce. I believe you can never add too much coriander to any Indian preparation. In fact, any amount can be added without fear of ruining the dish, something that can't be said about any other herb!

Coriander seeds: Small round seeds from the coriander plant, used in many Indian dishes. Roasting and grinding them just before using is the best way to release their flavour. Ground coriander seeds are often mixed with ground cumin seeds to form *dhania-jeera* powder (coriander-cumin powder).

Cumin seeds: Aromatically spicy rather than hot; a spice used for many centuries. Its flavour is released when lightly roasted in a frying pan before using. The roasted seeds can be ground in a coffee grinder or a pestle and mortar and the powder stored in an airtight container. Often used to sprinkle over yogurt dishes, such as *raitas*, and chutneys.

Curry leaf: The leaf of a tree native to India. When added to hot oil, curry leaves release a wonderful aroma. Used most often with vegetarian food, they are also used in fish and prawn (shrimp) curries. In Southern India, they are often combined with coconut. The dried leaves, which are available from Indian groceries, are a poor substitute. Fresh curry leaves can be stored for up to a week in a plastic bag in the refrigerator. Discard when brown marks appear on them.

Garam masala: *Garam* means 'hot' and *masala* means 'spices'. Cardamom, cinnamon, cloves and bay leaves all form part of *garam masala*. Sometimes fennel seeds are also added. *Garam masala* adds both flavour and aroma. I favour using whole *garam masala* (cardamom pods, cinnamon sticks, bay leaves and whole cloves) for cooking, and use the powdered form to garnish dishes just before serving. Generally used with meat and rice, though rarely with fish or vegetables, as the combination of powerful spices is considered too strong for delicate flavours.

Garlic: Popular the world over. One of the key flavours in a vast range of savoury Indian dishes. Puréed garlic can be kept in the refrigerator for several days.

Ginger: Derived from the root (rhizome) of the ginger plant and used for centuries as a flavouring and a medicinal cure-all. Puréed ginger can be kept in the refrigerator for several days, while fresh ginger will keep well for three weeks.

Green chillies: Available in a large range, they vary in the heat they generate! Fresh green chillies add a wonderful flavour to many dishes. If the chillies aren't too hot, you can leave the seeds in. If they are very hot, remove the seeds before using them or use them whole. They can be stored in a plastic bag in the refrigerator for up to a week. Fresh green chillies ground together with fresh coriander make a flavoursome paste, used as a base for sauces or marinades, known as *hara masala*.

Turmeric: The root of a plant from the ginger family, which is cultivated in tropical countries. The root is boiled, peeled, dried and ground. Retains its distinctive yellow colouring indefinitely but loses its flavour and aroma quickly, so should be bought in small quantities. Sometimes referred to as Indian saffron, though its spiciness is quite different to the delicate flavour of saffron.

medicinal benefits

The food we eat plays a vital role in the maintenance of good health. One leading nutritionist has even gone as far as to say that the right kind of food is the single most important factor in the enjoyment of good health, while the wrong kind of food is the single most important factor in the promotion of disease.

Bay leaf: Mixed with cinnamon and cardamom, is said to relieve respiratory congestion.

Black pepper: Said to burn toxins in the body and, together with ginger and chilli peppers, can relieve respiratory congestion.

Cardamom pods: Identified as having aphrodisiac qualities in that classic of Oriental literature, *Tales from the Thousand and One Nights*. Said to freshen breath and combat nausea, headaches, fevers, coughs, asthma, piles and eye disease.

Chillies: Astonishingly, eating hot chillies in a hot climate can help to keep the body cool, as they encourage sweating. Said to be good for digestive ailments.

Cinnamon: Cinnamon oil has been used to treat toothache and headaches, as well as impotence.

Cloves: Used since ancient times for medicinal purposes and employed to treat, among other things, toothache, fevers, dyspepsia and spleen, kidney, stomach and intestinal disorders. Has also been used as an ingredient in toothpaste.

Dill (fresh): used by the Egyptians, Greeks and Romans for medicinal purposes. According to the *Ayurveda* (Sanskrit writings in the ancient Hindu art of healing), helps to relieve gas, colic and hiccups and to control diarrhoea. Said to increase and medicate breast-milk to help strengthen a baby's digestion.

Garlic: Cultivated since prehistoric times and said to have been used by the builders of the pyramids in Egypt to keep up their strength. Reputed to cure many ailments, including nosebleeds, skin problems, coughs, colds, bronchitis and asthma. Said to dilate blood vessels and reduce high blood pressure. Often prescribed to prevent coronary heart disease. The list is endless and legendary. A libido booster, too, apparently!

Ginger: Excellent for counteracting flatulence, hence its use with lentils (daals) and cauliflower. Ginger is the supreme toxin digestant in the *Ayurveda* and, made into a strong tea with castor oil, is said to treat rheumatism and rheumatoid arthritis. The Ayurvedics used it to preserve food, as a digestive aid and as a spiritual and physical cleanser. It is viewed as an aphrodisiac in traditional Chinese medicine. Reputed to help with anaemia and liver complaints.

Onions: A trusted traditional home remedy. Said to protect teeth and to cure alopecia, asthma, laryngitis, heatstroke and rheumatism, among other ailments. Also regarded as an aphrodisiac and a symbol of fertility.

Peppercorns: The king of spices. Said to be particularly good for digestive ailments.

Turmeric: Has well-known antiseptic qualities. Said to slow bleeding when applied to wounds. Used extensively to improve the complexion and as a depilatory; also said to cure itching, skin diseases and conjunctivitis. Fumes from smoked turmeric are said to treat fainting, hiccups and asthma.

the final word

Clive Alderton Deputy Private Secretary to Their Royal Highnesses The Prince of Wales and The Duchess of Cornwall

Always know, examine and follow your own conscience.

Apply this simple test to seemingly complex problems and decisions, and it is amazing how straightforward they become.

Salman Amin President PepsiCo UK & Ireland

If you want to be a successful leader, make sure you listen. You can understand the motivations of others if you really listen to them. You can disagree with people, often vehemently, if you show them the respect of having listened carefully to what they said. The best way to build a coalition, or to ensure people follow you, is to open your ears and listen — if you do so, so will they.

Emma Arbuthnot District Judge (Magistrates' Courts)

To understand why sharing a bed with a – if she will forgive me for saying so – largish black woman changed my life, you must understand a little of what I was like before.

I was brought up in Chelsea by white parents. We lived and socialised within a white enclave and had no black friends. I went to the French Lycée in South Kensington, where I had few black acquaintances and was surrounded by racist jokes, which were not questioned by the mostly white schoolchildren.

Then, when I was at University, I went to Martinique in the French West Indies for my year abroad as part of a language degree.

I landed late one evening at Fort de France airport. Judith St. John, the daughter of a black Trinidadian father and a white Scottish mother, arrived on the same flight. We were to be language assistants at two schools on opposite sides of the island. We met that night as we waited in vain to be collected, and spent the night, head to foot, in a narrow bed in a disused classroom at the Lycée Schoelcher. That was the beginning of a friendship that continues, and will continue until one of us dies.

It was also the beginning of my education in the joys of diversity. I met black and Asian people from all backgrounds and formed lasting friendships. I learnt in Martinique that I shared their sense of humour, and on my return to England, I was struck, for the first time, by the isolation of my social circle. I have since attempted to encourage diversity amongst my friends and relations, because of the enriching effect that it has had on my life.

Jane Asher Actress, writer and businesswoman

I would never presume to give advice to anyone: life is so impossibly confusing and extraordinary that it's enough to try and get through it without doing any lasting damage to people or property. But I jot down here a few ideas that have helped me.

I've learnt to make lists: one of the few things I do manage to remember, at last, is that I won't remember things... If I write them down, even the most trivial, it helps to clear my head and stops them keeping me awake at night, trying to think of all the stuff I should be doing. Whether I ever manage to tick them off is another matter, of course...

You should never let yourself be put off pursuing subjects that interest you by well-meaning family or friends who may see them as limited in terms of your future: who'd have thought that my teenage hobby of cake decorating would eventually mature into my writing several books and running a business? Or that my love of reading and doing crosswords would prove so invaluable in learning the intricacies of the English language as to make me feel brave enough to tackle writing novels? If you enjoy something or have a fascination with it, you'll do it well and become informed and proficient at it, from bird watching to knitting. Whether it remains an enjoyable part of your leisure time or something that earns you money, it will be time well spent.

If I get depressed and upset, I do at least know now that it won't last forever: unless something seriously tragic has happened, such as the death or illness of someone I love, things look very different after a day or two. Everything changes, and a new day always brings a new perspective. I've learnt to try and hold off making any rash moves or precipitous decisions until my mood has returned to something like normal.

I never confuse my sense of awe and wonder at the universe with believing for a moment that it's a place of any real beneficence, altruism or equality. The human (and animal) condition is essentially a wretched one, and a large part of our nature is based on cruelty and selfishness. Once having realised this, I know I am surviving only by avoiding confronting the true nature of things; by looking away from the horrors that are happening at any one moment. This may sound desperately gloomy, but somehow this realisation is oddly comforting and puts life into some sort of perspective: we're all muddling along, making the best of it, and my tiny worries and preoccupations are of infinitesimal proportions in the bigger picture. I shall be gone within two or three decades, and will feel exactly as I did in 1782 – to pick a year at random. So – heigh ho – the fact that I've not yet emptied the dishwasher today is not going to prey on my mind.

HRH Princess Badiya bint El Hassan

When Pinky Lilani asked me to write something inspirational for her book, it made sense to me to begin by thinking of the most inspirational person I know: my father, Prince El Hassan bin Talal of Jordan.

He has taught me that everyone, regardless of ethnicity, gender or creed, has the right to live in peace and with dignity. The point is never to lose sight of the fact that we are all fellow human beings. No one, no matter what they do or where they are, is just a statistic, a faceless enemy or merely the 'other'.

As human beings, we must, and can, try to live in harmony with each other, and with the natural world we inhabit, for we are all part of God's creation. These are not simply fine-sounding words. Real wisdom and compassion inevitably lead to action. Throughout his entire adult life and much of his younger days, motivated by a sense of duty as a human being and as a Muslim, he has worked to improve the lives of others and to break down prejudice. Over the decades, he has done more than most, but there is always more to be done and it is this, rather than past achievements, that preoccupies him and spurs him on.

One of my father's favourite quotations is the following from the famous Muslim philosopher Ibn Arabi:

> My heart is open to all the winds:
> It is a pasture for gazelles
> And a home for Christian monks
> A temple for idols
> The Black Stone of the Mecca pilgrim
> The table of the Torah,
> And the book of the Koran.
> Mine is the religion of love.
> Wherever God's caravans turn,
> The religion of love
> Shall be my religion
> And my faith.

Ibn Arabi (1165–1240), tr. From *Tarjuman al-Ashwaq ;* also tr. As No: XI in the *Tarjuman al-Ashwaq: a collection of Mystical Odes, by Muhyiddin ibn al-Arabi, translated by RA Nicholson (London)*

Camila Batmanghelidjh Founder & Director, Kids Company

When I was 18, I had to be hospitalised in a US research hospital due to a severe endocrine disorder. The other patients on the ward were also there because of life-threatening and unusual conditions. During this period, I saw many people die. In fact, I was the only patient during that period to walk out of there alive.

When you are so close to the experience of death in such an intimate and inescapable way, you learn something very important: a profound understanding of how life is very precious but you as an individual are not that important. Some people might think this is a miserable thought, but it's actually hugely liberating. Whether you're poor or rich, famous or unknown, evil or good, you end up dying the same way and someone covers you up with a sheet.

It's an incredible equaliser, reminding all of us not to buy into our own or other people's pretensions and not to forget that neither wealth nor fame accompany you to the grave, so it's not worth making too much effort over silly things. This experience helped me access courage and cut out the garbage in my life. I measure every day by whether I'd be happy if today was the day to have the sheet pulled over me and whether I feel I've done enough to celebrate life, both mine and other people's.

Ultimately, if you're interested in legacies, the only thing left to treasure after your death is the kindness you've managed to share with others.

Sir David Bell Chairman, Financial Times (FT) Group

I think the easiest thing to forget in business – maybe in life in general – is to listen.

I learned this lesson again a little while ago in a role-playing session with a group of actors. They had a script, and the test was whether I would spot that one of them was the victim of very serious discrimination by his manager. If I let the actors talk, this fact would emerge; if I cut them short, it wouldn't. Well, I quickly 'got' the point of what I thought they were saying, skilfully (or so I thought) brought the conversation to a halt, 'solved' the problem and assumed that I had passed the test.

But I was wrong. In cutting them short, I never let them tell me about the discrimination and thus completely missed the point. Worse, one of my colleagues did the same exercise and 'got' it. In the debrief, I did not let on to her that I had cut them short. But I had.

It reminded me of something told to me by a headhunter. It involves a very simple rule first promulgated by St Benedict, the Italian monk who founded the Order of St Benedict in the fifth century. This, he explained, is one of the oldest continuously functioning organisations in the world, so its rulebook has to be worth something. Among his messages is this one: "Always listen to the young monks because they know all the things you have forgotten."

Time and again, I have also found this to be true. Of course experience, and a sense of history and the rest, is important. But it's so easy to think that's all that matters. Actually there is nothing quite like listening to a group of much younger colleagues talking about the present and the future.

So that's my piece of advice: always take enough time not just to listen but also really to hear what people are saying. Nothing yields a greater return.

Cherie Blair QC

Never open the front door wearing a nightie when the world's press are waiting outside.

Rosaleen Blair Founder & CEO, Alexander Mann Solutions

The best piece of advice I've had or could share would be simply to be positive in everything you do. I believe adversity can be the biggest source of opportunity, as long as you forget about the reasons why something wouldn't work and look at what it would take to make it happen. Turn any negatives you face on their head, and think about how those obstacles could actually help you achieve your goals. Then go out and do it!

Diana Brightmore-Armour CEO Corporate Banking, Lloyds Banking Group

There's a sign in one of our offices which says: Everybody brings pleasure to this office, some when they arrive and some when they leave!

As someone who plays multiple roles as a mother, daughter, sister, wife and CEO, I made the decision some time ago to focus on the former! I've learnt that a positive warm approach to people will get you further in life, whether it's the playground, home or the boardroom!

Fiona Cannon Equality and diversity director Lloyds Banking Group

I have been extremely lucky to have a number of mentors in my life, who have passed on the following:

Always have a life outside of work.

Never place responsibility for your happiness, career development or any other aspect of your life in anyone else's hands but your own.

Never be afraid to ask for what you want and be financially independent.

Shami Chakrabarti CBE Director, Liberty

I am anyone's equal but no one's superior.

Lyn Chambers

In thinking about what makes a difference in my life, I realise that it is about having a set of values and principles which guide me in all sorts of difficult or challenging situations.

I believe in being open to new ideas and people and not pre-judging outcomes or reactions. I try hard to be true to myself and to others, to be genuine and to practise what I preach without being too worthy. In order to do this, I need to remind myself of the following, even when it is hard to do so: be humble, always seek the learning from a situation and think positive.

I appreciate beauty in the world around me, and it helps me to remain calm. I take great pleasure in time spent with my family and friends and I try to instil the same values in my children – to be kind, to be open-minded, to be content and to take joy in learning.

Ian Chivers Director Finance and Corporate Services, NSPCC

When I worked for Merrill Lynch, I had the opportunity to work closely with the staff and students at a remarkable inner London girl's secondary school, The Mulberry School for Girls, where the students are mainly from the local Bangladeshi community. Together with the Tower Hamlets Education Business Partnership, we started a project that aimed to help the students better understand finance and entrepreneurship and to develop life skills.

With little prior interaction with Bangladeshi girls, I imagined they would be shy, retiring, possibly defensive and not interested in what we were trying to do. I was totally wrong. The girls were vibrant, confident, interested, eager to engage and have fun. The friendship they shared with me completely undermined my preconceptions and gave me an excitement about what can be learnt and achieved if we make the small effort to share time and talk.

We can't all be leaders and heroes, but we all have the opportunity to take small steps that can, in aggregate, lead to big changes, personally and for those with whom we spend our time. If you are like me, it's hard to venture out of your shell – but when you do summon up the courage, surprisingly good things can happen. Give it a try.

Elizabeth Coffey

My vocation is spotting people's hidden gifts – and nurturing individuals until they are ready to reveal them. So:

Dare to be

You have extraordinary talents, and with them you can lift souls.

Create your own shining identity, and light the world as a bold new star!

You are a precious gift to those around you, bringing joy and laughter. Your talents are manifold, blossoming even as the years pass.

Your genius rises as you believc in yourself and make the commitment that enables your gifts to flow through you and into our hearts.

This is a spiritual gift, which it is your sacred duty to cherish, love, feed and protect from all harm. With it, you can create magic.

You are a natural leader. This is an honour, and with it comes great responsibility: think carefully about where you will lead people and how it will affect them. The power in this role derives from the sacred trust that people put in you to love them and care for them as if they were your own children. Nurture a deep respect for this power and do not abuse it.

Embrace your leadership abilities; they won't fade because you ignore them or try to be 'just one of the gang'. This is part of your DNA: settle into your authentic, courageous and powerful self.

Your spirit is sunshine, sparkling and energising. We are blessed!

KG Dossani Indian Film Pioneer

The greatest inspiration in my life was my father, who was a humanist and believed in the value of every human being. Humanism is often accompanied by humility, especially when one understands the responsibility that humanism places on oneself to help others less fortunate and, thus, to make the world a better place. My father realised that this was a critical quality in life: if one has it, nothing else is necessary; without it, nothing else matters.

Secondly, my father exhibited great courage, whether it was in defence of his religious beliefs or in the defence of others. In political turbulent times during the Partition of India, he risked a great deal to save the lives of others.

Perhaps most interestingly he was always curious about life – in the richness of it and in building relationships that lasted for decades. Not surprisingly, the greatest assets he left for his family were the good will that was generated by his integrity.

So here is the real lesson from the life of my father: true wisdom lies not in well-chosen words but in deeds. Deeds that are done humbly, courageously and in friendship.

Shernaz Engineer CEO Verity Recruitment Group

My foster mother was a great influence on me and always said, "If you do someone a good turn or a favour, never expect anything back. This way, you will never be disappointed. If the good turn is returned, then it will be a surprise and a pleasure." I have always lived by this sage advice and have never been disappointed. It is simply wonderful if someone returns a favour.

Nicole Farhi CBE Fashion Designer

> There is no force in the world but love, and when you carry it within you, if you simply have it, even if you remain baffled as to how to use it, it will work its radiant effects and help you out of and beyond yourself: one must never lose this belief, one must simply (and if it were nothing else) endure in it.
>
> Rainer Maria Rilke, *The Poet's Guide to Life*

Rainer Maria Rilke (1875-1926), one of the great poets and philosophers of the twentieth century, wrote thousands of pages of correspondence. Among the letters selected and published, I love particularly *Letters to a Young Poet* and *The Poet's Guide to Life*. Their profound vision, of how we drive to create and understand, has provided the answers to many of the questions I ask myself. These books have been on my bedside table for many years, and Rilke's thoughts on how to live in a meaningful way accompany me always.

Heini Al Fayed

The one thing that I learned early in life from my paternal grandmother was moderation – moderation in our thoughts, behaviour and nourishment (body and soul). In achieving that, I suppose we would stay on a golden middle road of life. I fully understand that in today's world, where so many are looking for 'experiences', this is probably a very old-fashioned way of thinking.

Baroness Susan Greenfield CBE Director, The Royal Institution of Great Britain

I have several pieces of advice, all of them passed on to me by my mother, or just learnt from using her as a role model.

Firstly, a sense of humour puts everything into perspective and stops that otherwise corrosive obsessive circular thinking that can keep you awake at night. In particular, by laughing at people who may be trying to put you down, you are employing the most powerful weapon possible.

Secondly, to concentrate on the important things and people in life, and regard all else as nice to have, but not essential. I think this is particularly true in the current difficult financial times, when we can realise that merely owning things is not a guarantee of long-term fulfilment or happiness.

Thirdly, don't worry about what other people think of you, but what you think of yourself. Only you know when you are pushing your talents to the full, when you are being honest and when you are doing what is right. You can fool others but not the person in the mirror.

Finally, in the same vein, you have only one real rival – and that is yourself. There will always be people richer, thinner, younger, more attractive and cleverer than you are, but just remember, the reverse is always also true. Far better to focus on your own portfolio of talents and how to harness them to lead a happy and fulfilling life.

Larry Hirst CBE Chairman, IBM EMEA

I believe everyone is born with a chance to make a positive difference to the life of another Human Being. If you make a difference to one person, then your balance sheet is even; if you make a difference to more than one, then you are in credit with the stars.

Kelly Hoppen MBE Interior Designer

Never give up even if others do. To believe in yourself gives you a power to be who you want to be and to achieve greatness but always retain integrity throughout your life. And never stop laughing.

Mishal Husain News Presenter, BBC

My work has given me the privilege of hearing some extraordinary stories first-hand. In South Africa, I met the anti-apartheid activist Prema Naidoo at the Johannesburg Fort, where he had been imprisoned for playing a role in his country's freedom struggle. He came from a proud line of activists: in all, four generations of his family had been detained at one time or another. He took me inside the cell where he had lived in terrible conditions with 60 other men, most of them criminals, and endured hate, abuse and violence from his captors.

As he spoke to me, his eyes were shining; he never wavered, he never looked bitter, he never looked angry. I asked him how he could be that way. He told me that although he had forgiven, he had struggled on the two occasions when he had come face-to-face with his former interrogators. I told him I wondered what I would have done, had I lived in South Africa at the time. He told me of the many women who had been imprisoned in the Fort over the years, women like his sister and so many friends and acquaintances. But I was left with the lingering question – what *would* I have done? I hope that I would have had an ounce of the courage of people like Prema Naidoo. But I cannot be sure.

The Right Honourable Tessa Jowell MP

Minister for the Cabinet Office, the Olympics and London

Never take "No" for an answer if "No" is not the answer you want to the question you asked.

And remember, in our busy lives we are irreplaceable only to our children.

Baroness Helena Kennedy QC

Don't always follow the recipe.

Lady Gilda Levy Chairman, Women's Interfaith Network

My mother was a great influence on my life. Although she lost most of her closest family – mother, father, brothers and sisters – in the ovens of Auschwitz, she never taught me to hate. On the contrary, she took great pains to explain that sometimes the majority of people find it impossible to stand up to cruel and fanatical authority, and that it takes enormous courage to do so. I grew up with the deep belief that prejudice in any shape or form is totally evil and destructive. I have tried to define my life through fighting this evil, and to see all human beings as part of the entity that we call God. Each one of us has their own individuality in the Universe.

For my friend Pinky, whose friendship has enriched my life and who has, through her energy and enthusiasm, spurred me on to realise the path that I have to take – thank you.

Dame Julie Mellor

Glad I didn't listen to the young man at university who said, 'How dare you apply for the same job as me? You will get married and rely on men like me to look after you.'

The irony is, he is married to a wealthy fund manager who looks after him, and I have been the main earner in all my relationships. Sadly, this young man wasn't alone. Banks refused to give me the normal multiple of my salary as a mortgage because they too believed I would give up work and not be able to pay the mortgage. I found one bank that treated me differently, and I have been a loyal customer ever since.

Don't worry about a career path or what job is next. Work out what is important to you and what you want to contribute to society or the economy. Then you can take advantage of the right opportunities when they arise.

Azim Nanji Senior Associate Director

Abbasi Program in Islamic Studies, Stanford University

A little known Sufi saint was seen entering through the gates of the city and settling in a gulistan (rose garden) near the river.

The next day, he received a delegation from the well-known and established Master of the local community of Sufis. They came bearing a message in the form of a gift – a pitcher filled to the brim with milk, a signal that the Master's domain had no room for rivals.

The saint smiled, plucked a rose petal and placed it on the milk, saying: 'Tell your Master, there is always room for fragrance.'

Adapted from traditional sources

Junie Nathani

My family and friends make the difference – especially my five nephews, ranging in age from seven to 29. They keep me current and, dare I say it, sometimes even 'cool'! Each has a special place in my heart, and the time we spend together is always fun with many humorous moments. I remember the polite but barely concealed impatience at my first attempts on the Wii and their refusal to let me live down screaming on a roller coaster they reckoned was only for kids. I remember sitting in movie theaters, my raison d'être being to buy the tickets and hold the popcorn. I remember being impressed at the ease with which my new iPod was loaded and amazed at having an 11-year-old explain to me the finer points of Wagyu beef!

Vanessa Ogden Headteacher, Mulberry School for Girls

To Leon

There are many courageous, inspirational people in the world – women and men – who are role models for the young people I have care of as the head teacher of a large secondary school. Recently, I was drawn again to the life of a man who has inspired many young people through his work combating racism and stereotyping. His name was Leon Greenman and he died on 7 March 2008.

I first met Leon Greenman in 1993, when I was training to be a teacher. Leon was a remarkable and heroic man. He experienced the horror and terror of war and genocide as a young man during the Second World War. As a British Jew married to a young Dutchwoman, Leon was caught up in events in Amsterdam that led to the murder of his wife and young son in the concentration camps. He managed to survive in the camps through his sheer determination and the spirit of indomitability that characterised his life and work once he was liberated.

Leon's accounts of Auschwitz, where he spent some considerable time towards the end of the war, are deeply etched on my memory. As he spoke, he relived the time that he spent in the camps. The brutality, the pain and the sheer human evil he experienced defy expression. After his release, Leon dedicated his life to telling what happened in the camps: 'Never again, Auschwitz' was his declaration and he lived out his vow 'to tell' for the rest of his life.

Yet, despite his experiences in the face of such evil and suffering, Leon cut across the divisions of racism and social disharmony. Things that might have made a lesser person twisted and bitter, angered with humanity or alienated from society, served only to drive Leon onwards in his determination to change prejudice and dispel racism. He worked particularly with educators such as Ruth Anne Lenga at the Institute of Education and the Jewish Museum.

My pupils always listened to his compelling story with the greatest respect and admiration for his mission to go beyond race and faith and to see in all of us the common human spirit that binds us. Rabbi Dr. Jonathan Sachs once said that civilisations are built in schools. No one understood this better than Leon Greenman. There he fought his battle against racism and the horror that it can become. With the young lies the vision of what our future society can be, and in schools this is honed; Leon saw this and worked tirelessly to instil his passion for social justice with the young.

When Leon Greenman passed on, he left with all of us who heard him speak a responsibility to stand against genocide and the horrors of war, against every form of prejudice and discrimination. Leon was an inspiration to all my pupils and to me. ***Never again, Auschwitz.***

Mark Otty Area Managing Partner EMEIA, Ernst & Young

If I gain riches but lose those that I love, then I am poor,
If I have influence but don't make a difference, then I have
disappointed,
If I consider myself more than those around me, then I have
forgotten my own fragility,
If I live only for tomorrow, then I will wish for my time again,
If I speak words of truth, then I will rest peacefully at night.

Susan Payne CEO, Emergent Asset Management

Always Move Forward

People often speak about never giving up on their dreams, but a critical caveat is that failure is not a final destination. Being prepared and able to deal with it and move forward is fundamental to success in all areas of life. Something better may be waiting.

Never was this more clearly defined for me than when I was the Captain of Boats at McGill University, Montreal and aiming to be selected for the World Championships, 1984. Our four had trained twice a day, six days a week over two years to be selected by the Canadian team.

In May, just after we had returned from two weeks of water training time in Tennessee, where we had rowed for seven hours a day, one of the women on the team surprisingly decided that she did not want to continue, for personal reasons. With the reserve, we had a much reduced chance of making the selection.

As a result, and facing trials in July, I called a top boat club in Toronto, where I had also secured a job in a law firm, and asked if the club had a good four. I told the coach my aim – namely, to row at the Worlds in three months – and he thought me quite mad as I had no boat and virtually no time to prepare. Still, he kindly invited me to come and seat race. I moved to Toronto, sat on the dock and waited to be allowed into a boat with the aim, which I soon shared with the crew, of making selection in July.

Eventually, after several days and an ergometer test, I secured a place in the four, the members of which were prepared to race aggressively for several weeks; we soon shared the same vision and we won several medals. Finally, at the Canadian Championships 1984, we qualified for the Worlds in both the four and the eight. For me, this was a stark and, thankfully, early lesson about not stopping at obstacles when one has a realistic dream.

Success is easily as much about mindset and circumstances as about talent.

Richard Reid Chairman London, KPMG

The importance of understanding different cultures and backgrounds has never been more important. Success, in nearly everything we do, either personally or in business, involves people and working together, in order that we achieve the maximum benefits. In the current world economic situation, it is, in my view, even more important to work together, across the globe, than we have done in the past. Global travel has brought us all closer together, but we must all work hard to really understand other cultures to maximise benefits for us all.

Nabila Sadiq

Always give thanks for what you have.

Give love and be generous of heart; friendship is so important.

Treat others as you wish to be treated and be fair in all that you do.

Do not judge others; it's not our place to do so.

Help others improve their lives; in turn, yours will be improved.

Give freedom to whomever you can; it is, after all, the greatest gift of all.

Finally, smile and laugh out loud whenever you have the chance!

Jean Sharp Group Tax Director, Aviva plc

The three principles by which I live my life are:

i. To thine own self be true;
ii. We are all equal as human beings;
iii. Maximise return on effort.

In a working environment, these translate to:

i. I do not play office politics. If the emperor has no clothes, I will call it;
ii. I treat the Postboy and the Chief Executive with equal respect;
iii. My work/life balance is better than most.

Vicki Treadell British Deputy High Commissioner, Mumbai

My mother was my first role model (as is true for many women), and this is one of the best pieces of advice she gave me, which I now share.

Self-awareness is the first and hardest lesson to learn. If we don't know ourselves, how can we understand others? If we don't know ourselves, how can we make the most of the best of ourselves and improve the rest? Sometimes it is a bitter lesson to learn, but in that revelation you become liberated.

That is not to say it's easy or that you won't ever make mistakes. You will; that's life. But when you do, you will be equipped to understand why, in looking at yourself and in working out how to avoid the problem next time and to try to put it right this time.

And, in all this, it is OK to occasionally not to like what you see in the mirror or indeed to be very pleased with what you see as long as you understand who you are and what you are and try to make the most of it honestly and fairly and generously.

Vicky Tuck Principal, Cheltenham Ladies' College

Passion is no good without compassion.

I have learnt that it is important not just to do the right thing but to try to do it in the right way. I think passion, drive and vision are important, as are principles and values, but if you are to lead in a way that means people will follow, you have to set an example.

For me, this means poise, dignity, humility and stoicism. I haven't always modelled these attributes but I hate confrontation and anger and to lose self-control. Sometimes I have felt impatient, been dismissive of people who are not as passionate as I am, felt unsympathetic towards people who seem to lack commitment. I have learnt some lessons.

I hope I have carried many people with me, but I know that I have been particularly successful when I have been calm, polite, clear and gentle. You don't have to compromise in order to achieve your goals, but you have to respect the dignity of every human being.

Guilda Navidi Walker

My sister, who is a professor and my spiritual guide, introduced me to a passage that never leaves me night and day, from the Bahá'i Writings of Bahá'u'lláh:

> Strive, that your eyes may be directed towards the mercy of God, that your hearts may be attuned to His Wondrous Remembrance, that your souls may rest confidentially upon His grace and bounty, that your feet may tread the path of His good-pleasure.

Sir Nicholas Young CEO, British Red Cross

Making a difference, for me, is what it's all about actually. We have only one go at life (so far as we know!), and if you don't make it count in every way possible, then that seems, to me, a bit of a waste.

I worked 10 years in the law, mainly helping big companies get bigger – the money was good, my partners were fun, and the buzz that came from 'doing the deal' was exciting. But then two things happened.

First, I walked into my office one morning and thought, 'I'm going to be sitting at that desk dealing with their clients for the next 30 years: is that what I have really been put on this earth to do?'

Secondly, I met two great philanthropists of the twentieth century – Sue Ryder and her husband Leonard Cheshire. She had worked with the victims of the concentration camps after the war; he had been one of our top bomber pilots. They had both seen that you had a duty to fight against evil and wrongdoing, and that often meant sacrifice and risk.

Eventually, I went to work for them, helping them in their goal of setting up homes for sick and disabled people all over the United Kingdom and the world, feeling as I did so hugely privileged trying to help people who had far less than I did.

They gave me, and taught me, far more than I was ever able to give back to them – and helped me to feel, in a small way, that I could actually make a difference in the world. We all can.

index

A

Aesop
  on appreciation 15
  on kindness 16
Alderton, Clive 71
Amin, Salman 71
Anonymous 20
Arbuthnot, Emma 72
Asher, Jane 73-74
asparagus and coriander risotto 60

B

Badiya bint El Hassan, Princess 74–75
Bahá'u'lláh 93
bay leaf 64
  medicinal benefits of 67
Batmanghelidjh, Camila 75–76
Bejar, Hada 17
Bell, David 76–77
bhunaoing 62
black pepper, medicinal benefits of 67
black-eyed beans 51
Blair, Cherie 77
Blair, Rosaleen 77-78
Brault, Robert 18
Brightmore-Armour, Diana 78
Budgell, Eustace 18
Burke, Edmund 24
Buscaglia, Leo 16

C

Camus, Albert 17
Cannon, Fiona 78
cardamom 64
  medicinal benefits of 67
Chakrabarti, Shami 78
Chambers, Lyn 79
chicken
  with black bean, peppers and chilli 38
  pilau 58
chickpeas with spinach 43
chillies 65
  medicinal benefits of 67
Chivers, Ian 79–80
Churchill, Winston
  on enthusiasm 23
  on integrity 20
Cicero 15
cinnamon 64
  medicinal benefits of 67
Clark, Frank A. 17
cloves 64
  medicinal benefits of 67
Coffey, Elizabeth 80
Confucius
  on enthusiasm 23
  on integrity 20
  on kindness 16
coriander
  buying and storing 29–30
  culinary uses of 29
  as herb or spice 28–29
  history of 28
  medicinal benefits of 30
  nutritional value of 30
coriander-cumin powder 62
coriander leaves 64–65
coriander seeds 65
couscous, vegetable 47
Craik, Dinah 18
cumin 65
cumin rice 53
curry leaf 65

D

dill, medicinal benefits of 68
Disrael, Benjamin 15
Dossani, KG 81

E

Einstein, Albert
    on integrity 20
    on perseverance 22
Emerson, Ralph Waldo
    on appreciation 15
    on friendship 18
    on integrity 21
    on kindness 16
Engineer, Shernaz 81

F

Farhi, Nicole 82
Al Fayed, Heini 82
Feather, William 17
filet mignon à la Mikal 57
fish cakes 44
fish with charred garlic, pan-fried 59
Franklin, Benjamin 22
Fripp, Alfred 16
fusilli with chilli, artichokes and olives 34

G

garam masala 62, 65
garlic 65
    medicinal benefits of 68
    puréed 61
garlic spinach 50
Gibran, Kahlil 17
ginger 65
    medicinal benefits of 68
    puréed 61
green beans with cumin and garlic 55
Greenfield, Baroness Susan 83
Greenman, Leon 87–88

H

Helps, Arthur 16
Hill, Napoleon 22
Hirst, Larry 83
Hoppen, Kelly 84
Husain, Mishal 84

I

Ibn Arabi 75

J

James, William 15
Jowell, Tessa 85

K

Keller, Helen 24
Kennedy, Baroness Helena 85
Kennedy, Robert F. 24
King Jr., Martin Luther 24

L

Levy, Lady Gilda 85
Longfellow, Henry Wadsworth 19
Lyautey, Marshal 25

M

MacDonald, George 21
Mandela, Nelson 22
Marden, Orison Swett
  on generosity 17
  on perseverance 22
Mead, Margaret 24
Mellor, Julie 86
mince with spinach 54
Mother Teresa 24, 25
Mulcahy, Anne 21

N

Naidoo, Prema 84
Nanji, Azim 86
Nathani, Junie 87
Nietzsche 23
Nightingale, Florence 21
Nin, Anaïs 19

O

Oath of Friendship 18
Ogden, Vanessa 87–88
oil 62
omelette, spring vegetable 52
onions
  medicinal benefits of 68
Otty, Mark 89

P

Pasteur, Louis 22
Paterson, Samuel 19
Payne, Susan 89–90
Penn, William 25
peppercorns 68
pilau, chicken 58
Plato 16
Plautus 19
potatoes with cumin and tomatoes 40
prawns with creamy pasta 56
proverbs
  on appreciation 15
  on being the difference 24-25
  on enthusiasm 23
  on friendship 18-19
  on generosity 17
  on integrity 20-21
  on kindness 16
Proust, Marcel 19

R

Reid, Richard 90
Reiland, Karl 25
rice 63
rice, cumin 53
Rice, Norman B. 25
Riis, Jacob A. 22
Rilke, Rainer Maria 82
risotto, asparagus and coriander 60
Roosevelt, Eleanor 21

S

Sadiq, Nabila 91
salad of artichokes, olives and beans with pesto 49
salmon, teriyaki 37
Sawyer, Eve 23
Schweitzer, Albert
  on being the difference 25
  on kindnesss 16
Seneca
  on generosity 17
  on kindness 16
Sharp, Jean 91
Shaw, George Bernard 25
Smeltzer, Ruth 17
Socrates 21
soup, carrot and coriander 48
spinach
  chickpeas with 43
  mince with 54
spinach, garlic 50

T

teriyaki salmon 37
tomatoes, potatoes with cumin 40
Treadell, Vicki 92
Tuck, Vicky 92–93
turmeric 66
  medicinal benefits of 68
Twain, Mark
  on generosity 17
  on kindness 16

V

vegetable couscous 47
vegetable omelette, spring 52
Voltaire 15

W

Walker, Guilda Navidi 93
Ward, William A. 15
Wharton, Edith 19
Wilde, Oscar 16

Y

Young, Nicholas 93–94

The Difference To You

So, now you know what has made the difference for all those who are part of *Coriander Makes the Difference*.

What has made the difference for you? We'd love to know. You may simply want to give us your favourite quotation; you may want to remember the person who has meant the most; or you may want to describe the time you did something special which made you feel good and helped someone else. Tell us! Your contribution may just make the difference for another person.

To see what other people have contributed, and to contribute yourself, please visit our website: **www.coriandermakesthedifference.com**

And celebrate the difference!